To Mayim and Addy Love Love Tallulah @N6508a

African Animals
Rhymes & Recipes

Tracy Going

PENGUIN BOOKS

PENGUIN BOOKS

Published by the Penguin Group
Penguin Books (South Africa) (Pty) Ltd, 24 Sturdee Avenue, Rosebank, Johannesburg 2196, South Africa
Penguin Group (USA) Inc, 375 Hudson Street, New York, New York 10014, USA
Penguin Group (Canada), 90 Eglinton Avenue East, Suite 700, Toronto, Ontario, Canada M4P 2Y3 (a division of Pearson Penguin Canada Inc)
Penguin Books Ltd, 80 Strand, London WC2R 0RL, England
Penguin Ireland, 25 St Stephen's Green, Dublin 2, Ireland (a division of Penguin Books Ltd)
Penguin Group (Australia), 250 Camberwell Road, Camberwell, Victoria 3124, Australia (a division of Pearson Australia Group Pty Ltd)
Penguin Books India Pvt Ltd, 11 Community Centre, Panchsheel Park, New Delhi – 110 017, India
Penguin Group (NZ), 67 Apollo Drive, Mairangi Bay, Auckland 1310, New Zealand (a division of Pearson New Zealand Ltd)

Penguin Books (South Africa) (Pty) Ltd, Registered Offices:24 Sturdee Avenue, Rosebank, Johannesburg 2196, South Africa

www.penguinbooks.co.za

First published by Penguin Books (South Africa) (Pty) Ltd 2009
Reprinted 2010

Copyright © Tracy Going 2009

All rights reserved
The moral right of the author has been asserted

ISBN 978 0 143 026129

Photographs by Charles Heiman
Designed and Typeset by Susan Heiman
Illustrations by Kym Surmon
Printed and Bound by 1010 Printing International Ltd., China

I would like to welcome you to this magical journey through the wild African bush as we explore and learn about some of the many animals found across the African continent. We live in a wonderful world that we need to preserve for the future so I have chosen only vegetarian recipes.

This book is about the love of reading, the beauty of words and the magic of poetry. But it is also about one of the greatest pleasures of life: food. Making food is a wonderful outlet for creativity; it is an opportunity to show our family and friends how much we care about them. It is about breaking bread and sharing it.

That is why a percentage of the proceeds of this book are going to Child Welfare South Africa, an organisation that gives abandoned, abused and neglected children a chance to have a childhood in a nurturing, caring and loving environment. So thank you for buying this book and making a difference to someone out there whom you don't know.

Tracy Going

CHILD WELFARE
SOUTH AFRICA

Acknowledgments

African Animals Rhymes & Recipes is a journey from A to Z, a journey that has taken almost a year to complete. None of this would have been possible without the support and advice of my dear friends Karen de Waal, Allison Smith, Sue Grant-Marshall, Anita Kvalsvig, Estie de Vries and Frank Fouche. Thank you for all the months spent listening to my ideas and adding valuable input.

To my little ones, Ashleigh and David, for putting up with all the hours I spent behind closed doors. To my eldest son Chase for giving much needed youthful advice. To my wonderful husband Arnaud, thanks once again for believing in me.

This project has been about synergy, so a very big hug and thanks to my team:

Nicky Gibbs, a leading South African chef, who amidst her cluttered diary, her international competitions and numerous food shows, found the time to compile recipes and test the recipes I contributed.

Susan Heiman, a highly sought-after graphic designer who has lived and slept this project. Thanks to you for your commitment, unflagging energy, infinite ideas and relentless enthusiasm.

Kym Surmon, an exceptionally talented artist, thank you for all the long days you spent conceptualising, drawing and painting these wonderful illustrations. You deserve international recognition for your unbelievable talent.

Charles Heiman, a great photographer, a big hug to you for the hours you spent with one eye flat to the lens of your camera. Thanks for all your hard work and creative input.

Contents

Africa

The land of kings, queens and tribal chiefs
A place of ancestors and mystical beliefs
A land of oil, diamonds and plenty of gold.
A history of civilisation both young and old.

It is the cradle of the origin of humankind
The second-largest continent you will find
Full of great riches and yet so very poor
It's about music, dreams and great allure.

With majestic pyramids to the far, far north
Where willowy camels stroll back and forth
Over rock-strewn plains and rolling dunes
The Nile River whispers soft, gentle tunes.

Further south, the Congo River Basin lies
A bright sight of skies filled with butterflies
Home to ancient tribes and many a beast
Of which the king of the jungle is the least.

From the Sahara Desert to the Serengeti,
Wide open plains and wilderness so pretty
Thousands of animals trying to stay alive
Because it is home of the feared Big Five.

From darkening dusk to delightful dawn
The pulse from the heart cannot be torn
So many truths and stories gone untold
A magical animal kingdom we now unfold.

B is for big, burly, bold, brazen Buffalo
Treading where many others fear to go
Usually quite placid, meek and so mild
If cornered or wounded they get wild.

That is when they stampede as a herd
Oh what a deafening noise to be heard
They snort and charge, so dangerous
In a group they feel quite adventurous.

The strongest bull leads the big pack
And the weaker ones follow at the back
It's an ongoing fight to stay in the front
Because no one wants to be the runt.

They lie in the shade in the heat of day
And eat and grunt the long night away
They drink lots of water to feel better
Time now to make Buffalo Bruschetta!

Buffalo Bruschetta

This snack will have you charging through the rest of the day!

YOU NEED:

8 slices bread, about 1cm thick, cut from a crusty loaf
2 cloves fresh garlic
4 ripe tomatoes, roughly chopped
8 slices mozzarella cheese
Salt and pepper
Olive oil

HOW TO MAKE IT:

- Put a little oil into a hot pan, this pan must not be too hot as it will burn the bread
- Lightly toast until golden brown
- Then rub the bread with the garlic to give the toast a light garlic flavour
- Put a slice of mozzarella cheese onto each piece of bread
- Roughly chop the tomatoes and put them on the toast slices
- Season with salt and pepper and drizzle with a little olive oil and you have some yummy Buffalo Bruschetta!

TOOLS:

Bread knife
Frying pan
Chopping board
Plates

C is for completely crazy, cranky Crocodile
A so very advanced and prehistoric reptile
It's lived years of time and seen many wars
And dates all the way back to the dinosaurs.

They are so very good at their snappy hunt
As they tuck webbed feet behind their front
Swimming so fast, making very quick turns
Catching their prey which just never learns.

For crocodiles it is a day of great fun
Waiting for their prey out in the blazing sun
They rush out to strike and then do attack
With a sudden rush and very mighty whack!

They start so terribly cute, itsy-bitsy and small
Growing to be six metres large; big and tall
Beware of crocodiles, you might be lunch
Oh yes, we now enjoy the Crocodile Crunch.

Crocodile Crunch

These cookies will get your jaws crunching just like a crocodile!

YOU NEED:

½ cup sugar
½ cup butter
¼ cup cocoa
½ cup golden syrup
2½ cups cornflakes

TOOLS:
Measuring cup
Medium pot
Wooden spoon
Baking tray

HOW TO MAKE IT:

- Put the sugar, butter and cocoa in a pot, and melt together on a low heat
- Add the syrup, but be careful not to boil the mixture
- When melted and all mixed together remove from the heat and cool slightly
- Add the cornflakes and gently fold in with a wooden spoon
- When the cornflakes are thoroughly coated with the chocolate mixture, spoon into small piles on a baking tray and leave to set

D is for the delightfully ditsy and daft Duiker
So many different kinds found all over Africa
Usually alone and very seldom found in a pair
Frightfully timid and shy but always so aware.

You will find them in various shades of brown
And they're always jumping up, up and down
With front legs a little shorter than the back
They are ready to flee in case of any attack.

They eat buds, leaves and all kinds of seed
Following monkeys and birds dropping feed
Their alarm call is just a grunted nasal snort
A soft, gentle sound that's really quite short.

They run in a quick pattern of zig, zig and zag
That's when they're fleeing or just playing tag
They dash with a flash when they get a fright
I think you'll enjoy this light Duiker Delight!

Duiker Delight

This is a delightful and delicious way to end any meal!

YOU NEED:

2 cups fresh or frozen berries
1 slab white chocolate
1 slab milk chocolate
1 tub of your favourite ice cream

HOW TO MAKE IT:

- If your berries are frozen, let them defrost, then push them through a sieve with a wooden spoon into a bowl
- Break the milk chocolate into small pieces and melt it in a pan over a low heat
- Put two scoops of ice cream into each bowl, cover with berry mixture and break white chocolate on top
- Drizzle with melted milk chocolate
- Invite your friends and family to enjoy this Duiker Delight taste sensation

TOOLS:

Small pot
Ice cream scoop
Sieve
Wooden spoon
Serving bowls
Mixing bowl

E is for the extraordinary, enormous Elephant
With a great memory it is so vastly intelligent
Its greatest weapon is its hard protected tusk
Which grows all its life from dawn until dusk.

But the trunk is its most, most important part
To pick up blades of grass or tear trees apart
They listen with it carefully put to the ground
Raising it up as they sniff and smell around.

They flap their ears to look angry and cross
Letting other animals know just who is boss
Not that they always want to fight and duel
Waving their ears all day helps to keep cool.

It is the largest mammal to be found on land
Trumpeting and charging they are so grand
So big, grey and tough, it's a real super-sizer
Let's whip up a delicious Elephant Energiser!

Elephant Energiser

All the vitamins in this smoothie would give an
Elephant energy for the rest of the day!

YOU NEED:

1 cup berries
1 banana
1 cup vanilla yoghurt
1 cup ice

HOW TO MAKE IT:

- Peel the banana and slice
- Place all the ingredients in a blender and blend until very smooth.
- Enjoy your Elephant Energiser smoothie

TOOLS:

Blender
Small knife
Glass

F is for the fabulously feisty Bat-eared Fox
With a brown coat it wears long black socks
To the south and east of Africa they're found
Hiding in thick bush and holes in the ground.

A group of foxes is generally called a skulk
Often alone, foxes are seldom seen in bulk
He is sometimes called a dog, she a vixen
Little ones answer to cub, pup and kitten.

All foxes are known to be crafty and cunning
Doubling back on their tracks and running
What really sets this fox apart from its peers
Are its huge, cupped and incredibly big ears.

They don't like moving around during the day
As to hawks and eagles they are easy prey
And to be caught, oh what a frightful disaster
What do you think of a fresh Fox Frittata?

Fox Frittata

A healthy start to your day will keep you as cunning and crafty as a fox!

YOU NEED:

4 large eggs
50ml cream
12 cherry tomatoes
1 teaspoon butter
Salt and pepper

TOOLS:
Non-stick frying pan with a metal handle
2 mixing bowls
Whisk
Oven gloves
Spatula
Plate

HOW TO MAKE IT:

- Preheat the oven to 180°C
- Separate the egg whites from the yolks in two different bowls
- Whip the egg whites with the whisk until they form soft peaks
- Season the yolks with salt and pepper and add the cream. Mix well
- Fold the whites into the yolks
- Place the pan over medium heat and melt the butter
- Pour the egg mixture into the pan and arrange the tomatoes on top
- Leave on the heat for 5 minutes
- Place into the oven for 10 minutes
- Remove using oven gloves and eat hot

G

G is for the gentle and very graceful Giraffe
They are all so tall, even when born as a calf
The neck is so very long that in order to drink
They spread front legs so as not to fall nor sink.

The neck is really its most fascinating feature
Oh what a delightful and wonderful creature
It is easier to eat leaves and browse the trees
Without having to get down on knobby knees.

Each giraffe has its own unique pattern of dots
It's their strange way of walking that one spots
They run very fast but please not for too long
They kick really hard and are known as strong.

They're out in the sun and to avoid being stung
The creator has made a blue and black tongue
They don't sleep much, only two hours a day
Let's make Giraffe Giggles, what do you say?

Giraffe Giggles

This will keep any busybody strong in the heat of the day!

YOU NEED:

24 button mushrooms
1 box phyllo pastry
Olive oil
Garlic butter
Hummus dip

TOOLS:

Cutting board
Knife
Pastry brush
Non-stick baking tray
Paper towel

HOW TO MAKE IT:

- Preheat the oven to 180°C
- Wash the mushrooms and pat dry with paper towel
- Remove the stem and smear each mushroom with a little garlic butter
- Cut 24, 10cm squares of phyllo pastry
- Brush each square with a little olive oil
- Place a mushroom in the centre and fold the corners inwards to form a little parcel
- Place on the baking tray and brush with a little olive oil
- Bake for 20 minutes or until golden brown
- Leave for 5 minutes to cool and serve with hummus dip

15

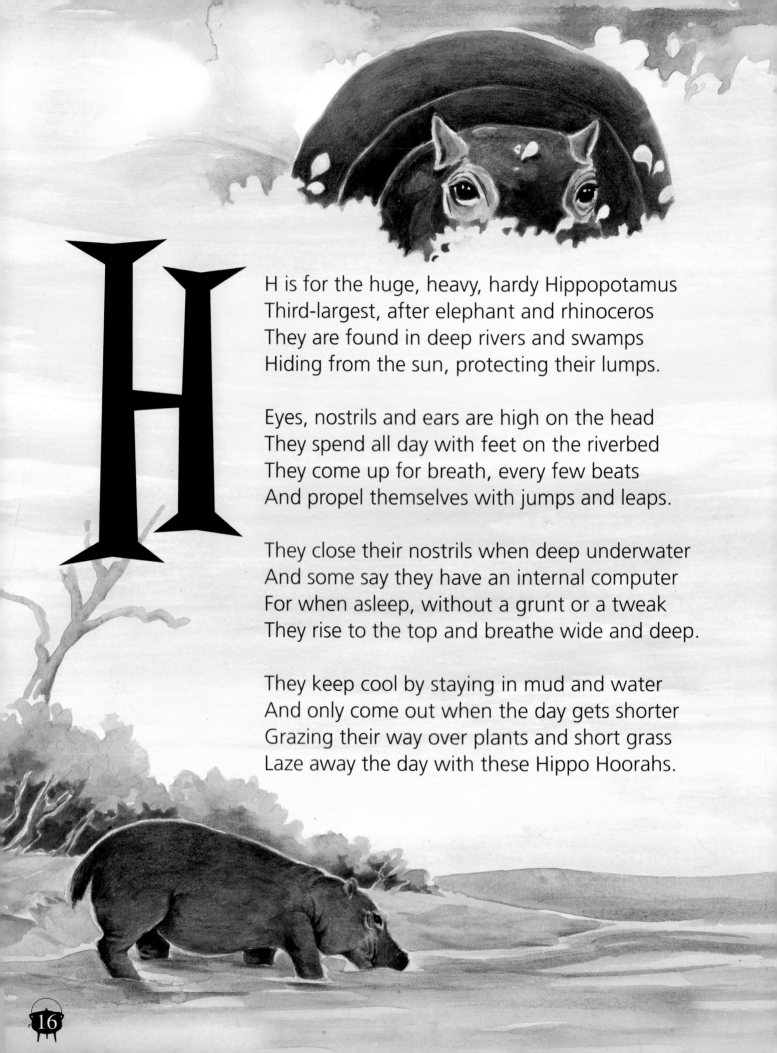

H

H is for the huge, heavy, hardy Hippopotamus
Third-largest, after elephant and rhinoceros
They are found in deep rivers and swamps
Hiding from the sun, protecting their lumps.

Eyes, nostrils and ears are high on the head
They spend all day with feet on the riverbed
They come up for breath, every few beats
And propel themselves with jumps and leaps.

They close their nostrils when deep underwater
And some say they have an internal computer
For when asleep, without a grunt or a tweak
They rise to the top and breathe wide and deep.

They keep cool by staying in mud and water
And only come out when the day gets shorter
Grazing their way over plants and short grass
Laze away the day with these Hippo Hoorahs.

Hippo Hoorahs

These meringues are great to boost your energy levels after a busy day!

YOU NEED:

2 large egg whites
100g castor sugar
100g of your favourite chocolate
Edible glitter

TOOLS:

Large bowl
Electric whisk
Non-stick baking tray
Small bowl
Small pot

HOW TO MAKE IT:

- Preheat the oven to 120°C
- Separate the eggs carefully so as not to get any of the yolk in the egg white
- Place the egg whites into the large bowl and whisk until they stand up in peaks
- Add half the sugar and whisk until the mixture starts getting stiff.
- Add the rest of the sugar and beat till stiff
- Pile spoonfuls on the non-stick tray
- Place in the oven for two and a half hours and the meringues should be nice and crisp
- Place 2 cups of water into the small pot and place on a medium heat
- Break the chocolate into the small bowl and place over the small pot to melt
- Drizzle the chocolate over the meringues
- Once set, sprinkle with edible glitter

I is for the interesting and impish Impala
An antelope just like Oribi, Oryx and Nyala
Impalas are active during the day and night
They're a sign that needed water is in sight.

With a glossy coat, a great chestnut brown
And its underbelly, a beautiful white gown
The tips of its little ears are a glossy black
With a long stripe all down its curved back.

With a unique scent gland found in the foot
They uproot themselves and don't stay put
As they roam very far over wide open plains
Following their own trail back even if it rains.

They hop and skip with no effort or reason
Especially during the long hunting season
With hearing so good they're very attentive
It'll be fun to make a light Impala Impressive!

Impala Impressive

This is an impressive way to end any delicious meal!

YOU NEED:

1 medium pawpaw
4 kiwi fruit
16 strawberries
1 bunch black grapes
4 granadillas

TOOLS:
Chopping board
Knife
Skewers

HOW TO MAKE IT:

- Wash all the fruit well
- Peel and deseed the pawpaw and cut into chunks
- Peel the kiwi fruit and cut into slices
- Cut the green off the strawberries
- Place the fruit onto the skewers
- Drizzle with the granadilla pulp

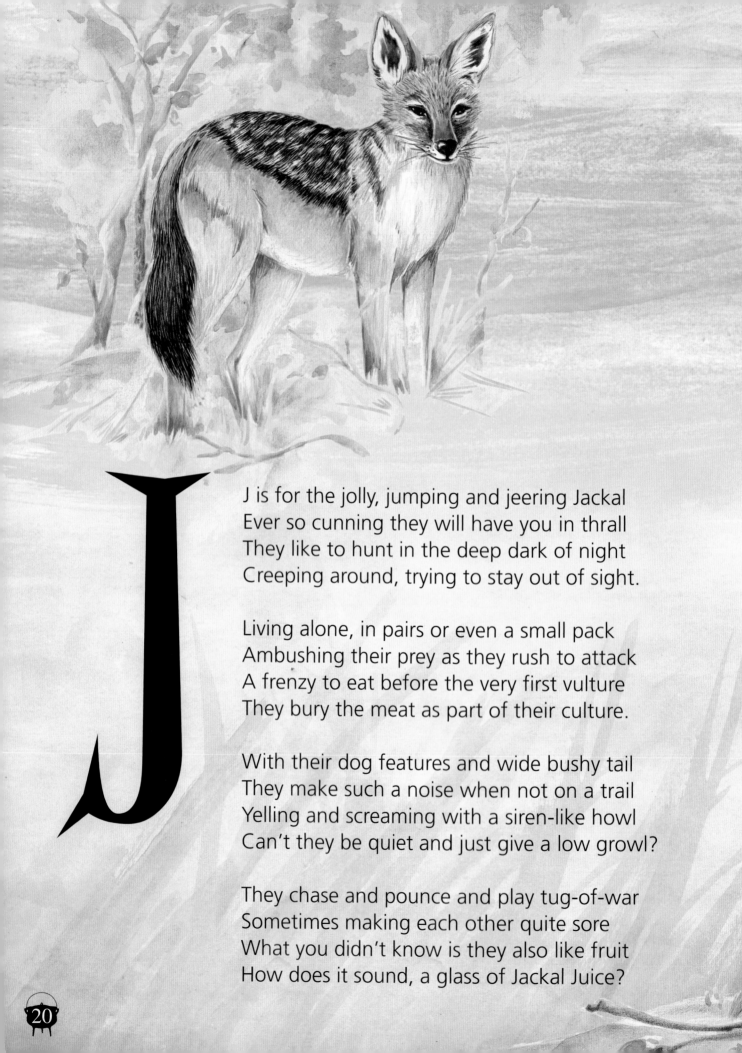

J

J is for the jolly, jumping and jeering Jackal
Ever so cunning they will have you in thrall
They like to hunt in the deep dark of night
Creeping around, trying to stay out of sight.

Living alone, in pairs or even a small pack
Ambushing their prey as they rush to attack
A frenzy to eat before the very first vulture
They bury the meat as part of their culture.

With their dog features and wide bushy tail
They make such a noise when not on a trail
Yelling and screaming with a siren-like howl
Can't they be quiet and just give a low growl?

They chase and pounce and play tug-of-war
Sometimes making each other quite sore
What you didn't know is they also like fruit
How does it sound, a glass of Jackal Juice?

Jackal Juice

This juice should have you chasing and pouncing from the very first sip!

YOU NEED:

2 cups grapes
2 apples peeled, and sliced
1 teaspoon freshly grated ginger
Juice of half a lemon
1 litre of sparkling water

HOW TO MAKE IT:

- Wash all fruit
- Blend apple slices and fresh ginger together
- Add the grapes and lemon juice
- Blend until smooth
- Mix with sparkling water and you will have the most delicious fresh Jackal Juice

TOOLS:

Vegetable peeler
Blender
Big jug
Small knife
Juicer

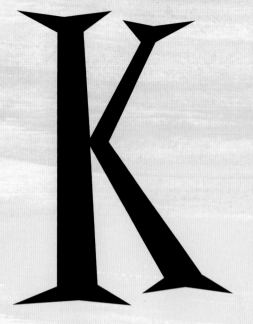

K is for the keen and kind, kicking Kudu
If it's difficult to pronounce just say koodoo
A male has two and a half twists to a horn
They're seldom used to fight, just to warn.

With a brown-grey coat it is so very sleek
You'll notice big white spots on the cheek
With a small V that runs between the eyes
All this part of a smart camouflage disguise.

Although light of foot, it's slow you will find
They bolt, then stop and then look behind
Eyes wide open and a look of total surprise
Finally running for cover without goodbyes.

They enjoy eating leaves, grass and shoots
And sometimes vines, roots and fallen fruits
As they gasp, grunt and cluck the day away
Let's make the Kudu Kiss, what do you say?

Kudu Kiss

This cheesecake is so light and fluffy, it's like a real Kudu Kiss!

YOU NEED:

1 packet digestive or tennis biscuits
175g butter
200g marshmallows
300g cream cheese
200ml fresh cream

TOOLS:
22cm non-stick cake tin
Blender
Small pot
Bowl
Spatula
Whisk

HOW TO MAKE IT:

Base:
- Melt 100g of butter in the small pot over medium heat
- Crush the biscuits in the blender till you have fine crumbs and add to the butter
- Place the biscuit mix into the cake tin and spread it evenly across the base. Allow to set

Filling:
- Melt the marshmallows in the rest of the butter over medium heat. Allow to cool for 10 minutes
- Once cool add half of the cream cheese and mix till well blended
- Meanwhile, whip the cream in a bowl using the whisk and add the other half of the cream cheese
- Pour the marshmallow mixture from the pot into the bowl and fold in with a spatula until evenly mixed
- Pour onto the biscuit mix in the cake tin to set
- Leave in the fridge for 2 hours

L

L is for Lion, so lazy, lanky, lofty and loud
So brave, courageous and awfully proud
Of all the wild African animals it is the king
What a wonder to the bush they do bring!

Males have a thick mane around the head
Filling those all around with fear and dread
It has huge shoulders and long sharp claws
And oh my, such powerful and vicious jaws.

When not hunting they rest, sleep and snore
Lazing about twenty hours out of twenty four
As they wake, they stretch and yawn so wide
Breathing in air and getting energy to stride.

Like all cats they have very good night vision
Which helps them hunt with great precision
A roar can be heard eight kilometres away
Let's get the Lion Linguine pasta under way!

Lion Linguine

This pasta dish will definitely get a roar of approval from family and friends!

YOU NEED:

500g linguine pasta
30g butter
1 packet mushrooms
2 egg yolks
150ml fresh cream
50g freshly grated parmesan
Salt and pepper

TOOLS:

Chopping board
Knife
Large pot
Large pan
Wooden spoon
Colander
Small bowl
Fork

HOW TO MAKE IT:

- Slice the mushrooms and fry in the butter until cooked
- Bring the water to the boil in a big pot. Add pasta and cook until ready. Pour out water using a colander and return pasta to the pot
- In a small bowl mix the egg yolks, cream and parmesan cheese together with a fork. Add some salt and pepper
- Toss everything together in the pot and serve immediately

M is for the mighty, mischievous Meerkat
Always so busy as they work, chit and chat
Fretting all day, tackling tasks and goals
Running down burrows, in and out of holes.

Slaving as teachers, guards and sentinels
Always on watch at the end of their tunnels
With their dark glasses around their eyes
They look to the sun watching for bad guys.

Because of danger, they're always on alert
High up on hind legs looking cute and pert
Balancing on a slender tail as they stand
Closing ears to protect them from the sand.

They can't retract their claws like other cats
So long and hard, perfect for foraging rats
Do you know that they don't need to drink?
Now for Meerkat Munch, what do you think?

Meerkat Munch

Meerkats don't need to drink as they get all the liquid they need from good, healthy food.

YOU NEED:

¼ white cabbage
2 large carrots
3 sticks celery
1 apple
1 red onion
¼ cup mayonnaise
4 tablespoons olive oil

TOOLS:
Chopping board
Knife
Vegetable peeler
Grater
Large bowl

HOW TO MAKE IT:

- Finely slice the cabbage
- Peel and grate the carrots
- Chop the celery
- Core and grate the apple finely
- Peel and chop the onion
- Mix the olive oil and mayonnaise together
- Mix all the ingredients together in the bowl and bind with the mayonnaise and olive oil mixture

N is for the nice, natty, naughty and nifty Nyala
For them you need to look harder and farther
So secretive and shy, seldom seen in the light
You'll be lucky to spot them in the dark of night.

He is so handsome with a black-haired throat
Not to mention his shaggy blue and grey coat
It's his high-fashion yellow stockings one sees
Hiding his dusty and dirty, big knobby knees.

She's rather quite fair in her reddish-brown suit
I think you'll agree they both look terribly cute
They bark as they run and then hide for cover
Through the dense bush so you won't discover.

Always near to water, as grazers and browsers
They feed on leaves and fruits, even flowers
Using horns or hooves to dig tubers and roots
Now for Nyala Nibbles as you put on your boots!

Nyala Nibbles

These Nyala Nibbles will keep you warm in winter!

YOU NEED:

8 tortillas
200g cheddar cheese
1 bunch spring onions
3 avocados
2 limes
Salt and pepper
Chilli sauce (if you wish)

TOOLS:
Large non-stick frying pan
2 small bowls
Grater
Chopping board
Knife
Fork

HOW TO MAKE IT:

Tortillas:
- Grate the cheddar cheese, chop the spring onions and mix together in a small bowl
- Put the stove on a medium heat and heat up the pan
- Spread the cheese mix on 4 tortillas and put the other 4 on top like a sandwich
- Place into the pan and cook until the cheese has melted

Avo dip:
- Skin and remove the avo pip and place the flesh in a small bowl
- Squeeze the lime juice over the avocados and mash with the fork
- Season with salt and pepper and add a little chilli sauce if you like

O is for the not so ordinary, opulent Ostrich
With wings so wide they're rather outlandish
They're the largest living bird on planet earth
But will never fly, being flightless from birth.

He is quite black and she is a greyish-brown
With feathers so soft, just a light fluffy down
Both have long necks and oh so bare thighs
With small, little heads and very large eyes.

They shelter their young under their wings
Covering their own legs when the cold stings
If scared they lie flat down against the ground
Hiding themselves, not seen nor found.

With long, powerful legs and four toes in all
They run great distances and so fast overall
Reaching speeds of seventy miles an hour
An Ostrich Omelette will give us that power!

Ostrich Omelette

This healthy herb omelette will have you running as fast as an Ostrich all day!

YOU NEED:

4 large eggs
2 teaspoons butter
Salt and pepper
1 teaspoon fresh basil
1 teaspoon fresh oregano
1 teaspoon fresh thyme
1 teaspoon fresh parsley

HOW TO MAKE IT:

- Whisk the eggs in the mixing bowl
- Over a medium heat melt the butter in the pan
- Add the eggs and cover with a lid to cook for 2 minutes
- Finely chop all the herbs
- Sprinkle with the herbs and add a bit of salt and pepper
- Fold the omelette over with the spatula
- Serve hot

TOOLS:

Non-stick
frying pan with lid
Mixing bowl
Chopping board
Knife
Whisk
Spatula

P is for prickly, precious, perfect Porcupine
Not so cuddly, but rather cute and quite fine
Best known as one of the African Small Five
They shelter in holes and caves to survive.

With a short browny-black coat that shines
They are covered in paler quills and spines
Raised by strong muscles just under the skin
They're used to poke predators on the shin.

To protect themselves they stamp their feet
And they growl and hiss, which is quite a feat
Raising the quills along the back and the tail
Shivering and shaking with a big noisy wail.

As they like to sleep through the whole day
They feed at night as they wander and stray
Scouting for roots and bark at which to gnaw
This Porcupine Pizza will have you in awe!

Porcupine Pizza

This Porcupine Pizza will have your quills standing up straight!

YOU NEED:

4 pizza bases
4 tomatoes
12 olives
1 red onion
1 green pepper
300g mozzarella cheese

TOOLS:
Non-stick baking tray
Chopping board
Knife
Grater
Bowl

HOW TO MAKE IT:

- Preheat the oven 180°C
- Chop the tomatoes
- Pit the olives and slice in half
- Chop the red onion into small bits
- Take the seeds out of the green pepper and chop into small bits
- Grate the cheese into the bowl
- Place pizza bases on baking tray and decorate with the tomato, onion, green pepper and olives
- Cover evenly with the mozzarella cheese
- Place into the oven and bake for 20 minutes

Q is for the quaint, quirky and quiet Quagga
That used to be found in the south of Africa
What a pity we didn't protect and conserve
It's now an animal we can't see or observe.

They have for so many years been extinct
With a sandy-brown coat they were distinct
The legs, tail and belly were a light off-white
I think you'll agree, they were quite a sight.

The darker stripes on its front we remember
Not too different from its cousin the zebra
Hunted for its skins and meat, it is a shame
We have no one else but ourselves to blame.

We need to look after wonderful planet earth
Saving plants and animals for all our worth
Let's do our bit for the world and plant a tree
As we make a Quagga Quiche for our tea!

Quagga Quiche

A light quiche served with a fresh green salad is always a hit on a lazy afternoon

YOU NEED:

1 packet ready-made puff pastry
Butter

FILLING:

1 bunch washed spinach,
stalks removed
3 large eggs
200ml fresh cream
Salt and pepper
100g crumbled feta cheese

TOOLS:

Large pot
Colander
Large mixing bowl
Rolling pin
Quiche dish
Medium mixing bowl
Chopping board
Fork
Knife

HOW TO MAKE IT:

Base:
- Make sure the puff pastry has defrosted
- Preheat the oven to 180°C
- Butter the inside of the quiche dish
- Roll out the pastry using the rolling pin and place into the quiche dish
- Using a fork, prick the pastry to prevent it from rising

Filling:
- Fill a large pot with water and when the water is boiling pop the spinach in for a few minutes to cook
- Drain the spinach in the colander and cool under cold water
- Squeeze all the water out of the spinach and chop finely
- Spread the spinach evenly over the bottom of the pastry
- Place the eggs into a bowl and beat with the fork
- Add the cream and the crumbled feta cheese with a pinch of salt and pepper
- Pour the egg mixture over the spinach
- Bake in the oven for 20 minutes
- Serve hot or cold

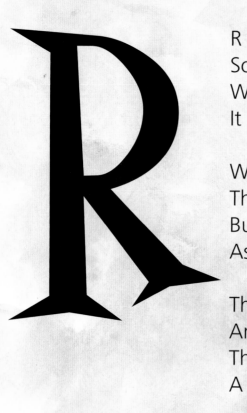

R is for the really rambunctious Rhinoceros
So big, bold and sometimes very boisterous
With an armoured body and a very big horn
It lumbers its way through bush and thorn.

With eyes so poor they can't see till too late
They charge first and only then investigate
But they do smell and hear what's around
As they swivel their ears to focus on sound.

The Black Rhino eats with a hooked upper lip
And is quite aggressive when it loses its grip
The White Rhino has a square lip to graze
A shoulder hump and much friendlier ways.

And as big as they are, they run so very fast
Bursting with sound as they do charge past
Sadly they are both on the endangered list
Now for Rhino Rice Noodle Relish with a twist!

Rhino Rice Noodle Relish

A real treat to keep you charging through the rest of your day!

YOU NEED:

1 packet rice noodles
1 packet baby corn
1 packet mange tout
2 red peppers
1 packet bean sprouts
2 teaspoons chopped mint
1 bunch spring onions

DRESSING:

1 chilli seeded (optional)
5 teaspoons sesame oil
1 teaspoon sugar
1 lime, juiced
2 teaspoons soy sauce

HOW TO MAKE IT:

- Place the noodles into a large bowl and cover with boiling water
- When the noodles are soft drain the water through the colander and leave to cool
- Wash all the vegetables well and chop them
- Place the noodles into the serving bowl and mix with the vegetables
- Mix the dressing together in a small bowl
- Pour the mixture over the salad and mix well

TOOLS:

Chopping board
Knife
Large bowl
Small bowl
Serving bowl
Kettle full of hot water
Colander

S is for the small, slight, slender Serval
A cousin of the golden cat and caracal
With very long legs and a fairly short tail
And freckled spots they are a tawny pale.

With large oval ears that hear so well
They're very good hunters which is swell
Standing so still with both eyes shut tight
Listening for rodents that are out of sight.

Chasing after hares, rats, birds and frogs
Digging in holes, burrows and under logs
Known to climb trees and even to swim
Pouncing and hopping at each tiny whim.

The human is its most frightening threat
All for its fur for the very fashionable set
They have to be careful of eating too fast
Chew your Serval Surprise, but make it last!

Serval Surprise

Chew well on this cucumber and pineapple salad and enjoy it!

YOU NEED:

1 large pineapple
1 large cucumber
1 bunch mint
1 red pepper
2 limes, juiced
100g cashew nuts
3 teaspoons sesame oil
Salt and pepper

TOOLS:
Chopping board
Teaspoon
Large bowl
Serving bowl
Knife

HOW TO MAKE IT:

- Peel and dice the pineapple
- Wash the cucumber and cut long ways.
  Remove the seeds with a teaspoon and slice thinly
- Remove the mint leaves from the bunch, wash and chop
- Remove the seeds and finely dice the red pepper
- Place all the chopped vegetables and fruit into the large
  bowl add the cashew nuts
- Season with the lime juice. Add the sesame oil and some
  salt and pepper
- Mix well and place into the serving bowl

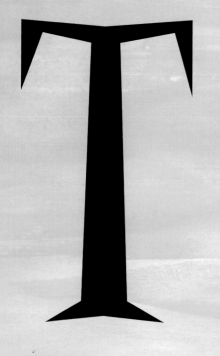

T is for the Tortoise, so tender and tame
It's a big, hard shell for which it has fame
The Sulcata is the third-largest in creation
But sadly not many left of this generation.

Its protective shell is its greatest weapon
Under which it hides for daily protection
Used to ram others when scared or cross
Knocking them over and winning the toss.

They might look big, lazy and so very slow
But they are always ready to move and go
Before you know it, look or turn around
Not a tortoise to be seen, heard or found!

They live so long and become so very old,
Up to one hundred and fifty years I'm told!
They graze and forage all through the day
Here comes the Tortoise Tart, make way!

Tortoise Tarts

Tortoises love to eat all day, especially anything colourful like tomatoes, strawberries or apricots.

YOU NEED:

200g flour
100g soft butter
1 tin apricots
1 jar apricot jam
1 teaspoon water

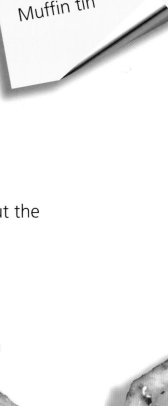

TOOLS:
Wooden spoon
Big bowl
Table knife
Rolling pin
Muffin tin

HOW TO MAKE IT:

- Rub the flour and butter between your fingers until the mixture is evenly mixed
- Add a tablespoon of water and mix till a doughy lump
- Set aside for 20 minutes
- Preheat the oven to 180°C
- Sprinkle some flour onto the chopping board and roll out the pastry till 3mm in thickness
- Cut pastry into rounds and place into the muffin tin
- Prick each a few times with a fork
- Put an apricot half into each round
- Bake for 20 minutes
- Allow to cool then remove the tarts from the tray with a table knife and set them on the wire cooler
- Brush each tart with the apricot jam and leave till they are well cooled

MORE TOOLS:
8cm cutter
Wire cooler
Chopping board
Pastry brush
Fork

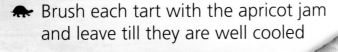

U

U is for, Ugandan Kob so utterly urbane
Slight like Impala but not quite the same
So handsome with a reddish-brown pelt
And white-ringed eyes they are so svelte.

Males use their horns to slash and clash
Fighting others with a resounding crash
Marking the space with a piercing whistle
They dash and dart around as they bristle.

Afraid of lions, leopards and hunting dogs
Leaping, they bounce over rocks and logs
Taking refuge in water and wet reed beds
A good camouflage thanks to their threads.

With big white ears and a bib on the throat
What an unusual and unique trenchcoat
For Uganda the land it's the national buck
It's a Ugandan Kob Upender, what luck!

Ugandan Kob Upender

This delightful upside-down pineapple pudding will have
you facing the day the right way up!

YOU NEED:

100g self-raising flour
1 teaspoon baking powder
100g soft butter
100g castor sugar
2 large eggs
25ml milk
1 tin pineapple rings
½ cup syrup

TOOLS:
Ovenware
baking dish
Baking paper
Bowl
Wooden spoon
Serving dish
Scales
Sieve

HOW TO MAKE IT:

- Preheat the oven to 180°C
- Sift the flour and the baking powder into the bowl
- Add the butter, eggs, castor sugar and milk, and beat till smooth
- Line the ovenware dish with the baking paper
- Cover the bottom with the pineapple rings and pour over the syrup
- Then carefully pour the cake mixture on top
- Bake for 40 minutes till golden brown
- Flip over carefully onto a serving dish so that the pineapples are on top. Peel off the baking paper and you can eat this either hot or cold

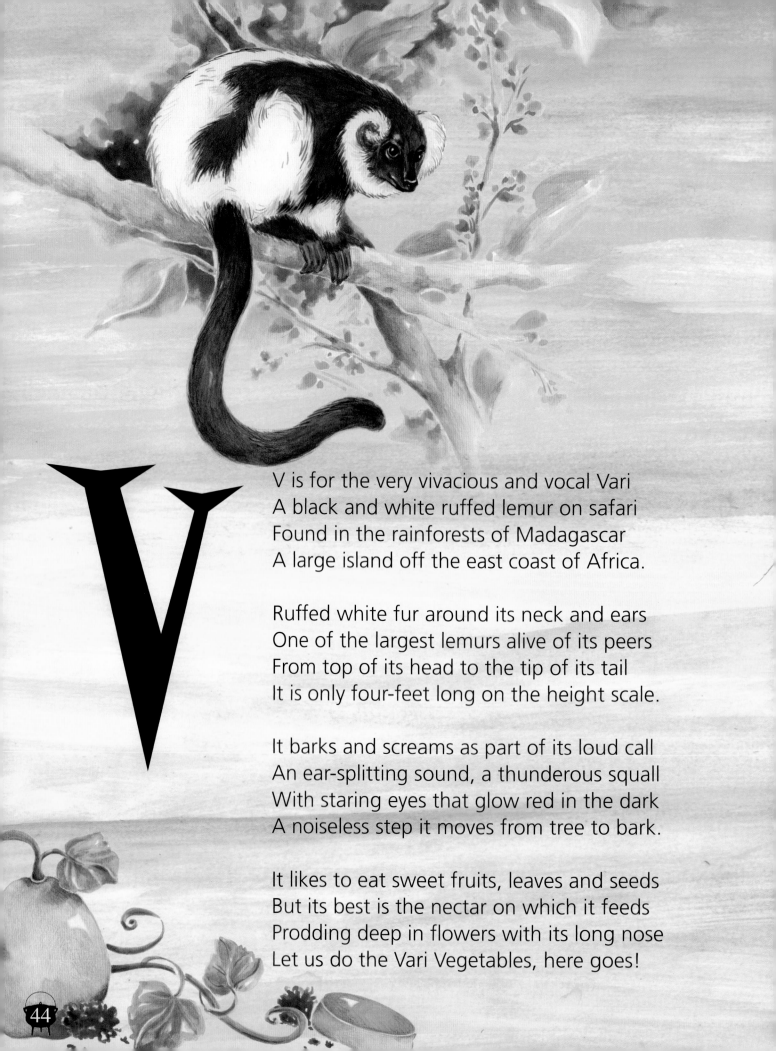

V is for the very vivacious and vocal Vari
A black and white ruffed lemur on safari
Found in the rainforests of Madagascar
A large island off the east coast of Africa.

Ruffed white fur around its neck and ears
One of the largest lemurs alive of its peers
From top of its head to the tip of its tail
It is only four-feet long on the height scale.

It barks and screams as part of its loud call
An ear-splitting sound, a thunderous squall
With staring eyes that glow red in the dark
A noiseless step it moves from tree to bark.

It likes to eat sweet fruits, leaves and seeds
But its best is the nectar on which it feeds
Prodding deep in flowers with its long nose
Let us do the Vari Vegetables, here goes!

Vari Vegetables

Nothing beats the fresh goodness of a delicious vegetable dish!

YOU NEED:

6 large potatoes, sliced
2 large onions, sliced
1 medium butternut, peeled and sliced
½ cup freshly chopped parsley
300ml fresh cream
100g grated cheddar cheese
Salt and pepper

TOOLS:

Ovenware dish
Chopping board
Knife
Vegetable peeler
Grater

HOW TO MAKE IT:

- Layer the potato, onion and butternut, sprinkling the chopped parsley between the layers
- Also between the layers add some salt and pepper (not too much)
- Preheat the oven to 180°C
- Cover with the cream and sprinkle the grated cheese on top
- Bake until the potatoes are soft, for about 45 minutes

W is for the wandering, weathered Warthog
An African swine, a rather wild wicked hog
In various shades of black, grey or brown
Its coarse, bristly coat is no elegant gown.

They might look savage and terribly fierce
They'd rather run than fight, stab or pierce
The tusks are there for more than just show
The warts protect from any attacking blow.

Their eyesight is not very good, with that said
Probably as they're on the sides of the head
They bullet and bolt around at a high speed
A quick, running start from danger, indeed.

To eat they kneel down on bent front legs
Snouting and shovelling for nature's dregs
All part of the mad feeding frenzy one sees
Let's make a Warthog Wrap, what a breeze!

Warthog Wrap

You'll have your own feeding frenzy with this wonderfully healthy meal!

YOU NEED:

1 ripe avocado
200g halloumi cheese
200g hummus
1 crispy iceberg lettuce
1 punnet cherry tomatoes
4 tortilla wraps
Olive oil

TOOLS:
Chopping board
Spatula
Knife
Frying pan

HOW TO MAKE IT:

- Slice the halloumi cheese into 8 strips
- Heat the frying pan over a medium heat and add a little olive oil
- Fry the halloumi until it is golden brown
- Peel and cut the avocado into 8 segments
- Finely slice the lettuce into strips
- Cut the cherry tomatoes into quarters
- Smear the tortilla wraps evenly with the hummus using the spatula
- Evenly divide the rest of the ingredients onto the wraps
- Roll up and eat

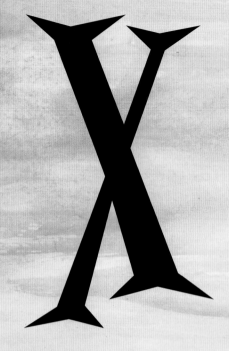

X is for eXciting and eXtraordinary Xerus
A ground squirrel's science name or genus
From a distance they look so fluffy and cute
But their coat is actually a short, bristly suit.

A brown or red-grey they are quite a sight
With big, round eyes ringed in bright white
Its tummy and inner legs are a soft vanilla
A speckled bushy tail used as an umbrella.

Sunbathing with bellies flat on the ground
Arms and legs are stretched out all around
To cool themselves they lie flat in the shade
Flicking sand on the back, the tail a spade.

Look carefully and you'll see no outer ear
But they have no problem to listen or hear
Unlike other squirrels they don't climb trees
For Xerus eXtras you'll say, more please!

Xerus eXtras

A most delicious way to nibble the afternoon away!

YOU NEED:

1 bag plain corn chips
2 large tomatoes, chopped
1 large onion, chopped
1 tub guacamole
1 tub sour cream
150g grated cheddar cheese

TOOLS:
Large ovenware dish
Chopping board
Knife
Grater

HOW TO MAKE IT:

- Preheat the oven to 180°C
- Lay the corn chips in the ovenware dish
- Cover with the grated cheese
- Place in the oven for about 10 minutes
- Mix the tomatoes and onion
- Take the chips out of the oven when the cheese is melted
- Place the tomato and onion mix, guacamole and sour cream on the hot chips
- A great snack any time of day

Y

Y is for, yelping, yowling Yellow Baboon
Always smacking its lips, what a buffoon
A pointed nose and hairless face so black
Strong jaws and heavy eyebrows so slack.

With a tail almost as long as its slim trunk
And yellow-grey fur, a good looking hunk
Walking great distances over the ground
Hiding in trees not seen, heard nor found.

Otherwise it's a very big noise from dawn
Barking and yelling, they grunt and yawn
Baboons drink water, each day they prefer
If not they lick the night dew from their fur.

Being rather intelligent and crafty of mind
Baboons will eat whatever food they find
Roots and fruits are best as a rule of thumb
Let's make the Yellow Baboon Yum-Yum!

Yellow Baboon Yum-Yum

Baboons love tubers and roots; potatoes give you lots of energy!

YOU NEED:

4 large baking potatoes
4 sprigs thyme
4 spring onions
100g butter
100g grated cheddar cheese
Salt and pepper

TOOLS:
Chopping board
Knife
Grater
Foil

HOW TO MAKE IT:

- Preheat the oven to 180°C
- Wash the potatoes well and wrap in the foil (dull side out as the shiny side reflects the heat)
- Bake for 45 minutes or until soft
- Chop the thyme and the spring onions and mix with the grated cheese
- When the potato is baked, remove the foil, cut and halve and smear with butter
- Season with some salt and pepper
- Cover with the chopped thyme, spring onions and the grated cheese
- Enjoy!

Z is for the zooty, zany and zippy Zorilla
A striped polecat, not a type of gorilla
It has long black fur and a very soft coat
Thick white stripes, except on its throat.

With stubby legs and a very long snout
A springy, fast trot when out and about
Often alone, it loves to wade and swim
It never climbs trees or is seen on a limb.

With sturdy claws on the feet, I do say
Perfect for stalking and pouncing its prey
If alarmed it raises the hair on its back
Lifting its tail, looking bigger on attack.

If scared enough, a smelly fluid it will spray
Enough to ruin any lurking enemy's day
It hunts at night and in the day it will rest
To end this book we make a Zorilla Zest!

Zorilla Zest

This Zorilla Zest will add zing to any light lunch!

YOU NEED:

5 juicy lemons
1 litre soda water
4 teaspoons castor sugar or fructose
Fresh mint

HOW TO MAKE IT:

- Cut 4 of the lemons in half and squeeze all the juice out
- Add the sugar to the lemon juice
- Combine with the soda water
- Cut the last lemon into slices and add to the juice
- Pop in the fresh mint
- Pour into the glass jug
- Serve and enjoy!

TOOLS:

Juicer
Chopping board
Knife
Glass jug

53

Interesting facts

Buffalo – To support their large bodies, buffalo have very heavy legs. Their front hooves are larger than those at the back because of all the weight they carry in their huge neck and head.

Crocodile – The crocodile has two stomachs, one of which usually has stones in it. This assists the crocodile to crush its food. If a croc loses a tooth it quickly grows another one.

Duiker – The duiker avoids predators by lying quietly or freezing motionless and dashing away at the last moment if approached too closely. The male takes no part in looking after its young, but both the male and female will respond if a calf is in distress.

Elephant – The elephant has no natural predator, only man, although lions may take calves or weak individuals. It is easy to tell whether an elephant is left- or right-tusked: the one tusk will be more worn down than the other.

Fox – One unusual characteristic about the bat-eared fox is its teeth: it can have up to 50 teeth. Males participate in guarding, grooming and playing with the young just as much as the mother.

Giraffe – The giraffe is the tallest animal in the world and a newborn giraffe is about 1.8 metres tall when it is born.

Hippopotamus – Baby hippos are born under water and their mothers help them to the surface of the water after they are born. The hippo usually stays under the water for about four to six minutes before coming up for air. Although they spend most of their time in the water, they are too heavy to swim.

Impala – The female impala usually only gives birth to one baby at a time. Impala are known for their jumping abilities and can jump about 3 metres high and about 9 metres forward.

Jackal – Jackals mate for life. They kill small prey with a bite to the back of the neck or they might shake them to death. Jackals are very vocal but they use a particular call when communicating with their family.

Kudu – The hierarchy among kudu males is usually determined by age and size. The males engage in sparring contests: they approach each other slowly, lock horns and push until the weaker one gives up.

Lion – Male lions only stay in the pride if they are strong enough to defend and protect the pride from other males. They are the only cats that live in large family groups.

Meerkat – Meerkats eat scorpions by quickly biting off the sting and then eating the rest. When they wake up in the morning they all come out of their burrows and stand around as they catch some of the sun's rays.

Nyala – The nyala is a spiral-horned dense-forest animal found in South Africa and is seldom seen in open spaces. They live alone or are sometimes seen in small family groups of up to 10 members.

Ostrich – The ostrich is the fastest-running member of the bird family. They are true dinosaurs with skeletons and fossils having been found that date back to over 120 million years. The ostrich can lay five to twenty eggs at a time.

Porcupine – When a porcupine loses a quill it grows another one. They live in holes that have been dug by other animals, but can also dig their own. The young leave their homes for the first time when they are about two weeks old, that is, after the quills which are soft at birth have begun to harden.

Quagga – The quagga's name comes from the sound it used to make. The last quagga died in late 1800s in the Amsterdam zoo. They were apparently very tame in captivity and it has been reported they were used as guards to look after horses and sheep.

Rhinoceros – A rhino can sleep either standing or lying down. The skin of a rhino is very sensitive, particularly to insect bites and sunburn. They are more active during the night and early morning than they are during the day.

Serval – The serval can apparently hear a rodent in its natural environment from about 6 metres away. They make a very distinct noise that sounds like 'how-how-how'. I think you'll agree they do look a bit like miniature cheetahs.

Tortoise – Although the Sulcata tortoise lives in an arid region it does require constant access to water. Out in the wild they dig long tunnels in order to avoid getting dehydrated.

Ugandan Kob – The Ugandan kob is not protected and is found in large numbers throughout its range. Unfortunately though, that range is shrinking. By eating grasses, kobs help keep the plains in a state of regrowth.

Vari – Unlike other primates the ruffed lemur doesn't carry its young on its back or on its stomach. A female gives birth and leaves her young in a nest made from twigs, leaves and vines. The nest is about 10m – 20m off the ground.

Warthog – The warthog is the only pig able to live without water for several months of the year. It has a higher-than-normal body temperature and it is believed this enables the warthog to conserve moisture in its body instead of using the moisture to cool itself down.

Xerus – The ground squirrel is active during the day and comes out of its burrow about an hour after sunrise in the summer and half an hour later in winter. It is not so active when it is wet and windy, and stays underground during sandstorms.

Yellow Baboon – Baboons travel in very large groups and anywhere from 8 to 200 are found in a troop. The strong males lead in the front, the females and babies are found in the middle and the weaker males follow at the back.

Zorilla – The zorilla is one of the smelliest animals found on earth. Although it isn't particularly big or vicious, it doesn't have many natural enemies because it stinks so much that other animals would rather stay away from it.